KU-453-006

My World of Science

SMOOTH AND ROUGH

Angela Royston

www.heinemann.co.uk/library
Visit our website to find out more information about **Heinemann Library** books.

To order:
☎ Phone 44 (0) 1865 888066
🖹 Send a fax to 44 (0) 1865 314091
🖥 Visit the Heinemann Bookshop at www.heinemann.co.uk/library to browse our catalogue and order online.

First published in Great Britain by Heinemann Library, Halley Court, Jordan Hill, Oxford OX2 8EJ, part of Harcourt Education.

Heinemann is a registered trademark of Harcourt Education Ltd.

Editorial: Andrew Farrow and Dan Nunn
Design: Jo Hinton-Malivoire and
    Tinstar Design Limited (www.tinstar.co.uk)
Picture Research: Maria Joannou and Sally Smith
Production: Viv Hichens

Originated by Blenheim Colour Ltd
Printed and bound in China by
    South China Printing Company

ISBN 0 431 13737 4
07 06 05 04 03
10 9 8 7 6 5 4 3 2 1

British Library Cataloguing in Publication Data
Royston, Angela
Smooth and rough. – (My world of science)
1. Surface roughness – Juvenile literature
I. Title
620.1'1292

A full catalogue record for this book is available from the British Library.

Acknowledgements
The publishers would like to thank the following for permission to reproduce photographs:
Alamy Images p. **19**; Chris Honeywell pp. **4**, **22**; Gareth Boden p. **21**; Network Photographers p. **20**; Oxford Scientific Films p. **6**; Photodisc pp. **8**, **18**; Pictor International pp. **16**, **23**; Robert Harding pp. **9** (Raj Kamal), **29**; Trevor Clifford pp. **5**, **7**, **10**, **11**, **12**, **13**, **14**, **15**, **17**, **25**, **26**, **27**, **28**; Trip/H. Rogers p. **24**.

Cover photograph reproduced with permission of Trevor Clifford.

Every effort has been made to contact copyright holders of any material reproduced in this book. Any omissions will be rectified in subsequent printings if notice is given to the publishers.

Contents

Any words appearing in the text in bold, **like this**,
are explained in the Glossary.

What is smooth?

These marbles are smooth. They have no cracks in them and no tiny dips or bumps. The **surface** of smooth things is completely even.

You can tell if something is smooth by feeling it. If you run your fingers across the cover of this book, it will also feel smooth.

What is rough?

This stone is rough. Feel a rough stone with your fingers. You will be able to feel the bumps, cracks and dips in its **surface**.

These things all feel rough. Some things are rougher than other things. The doormat is rougher than the school bag. The **bark** is the roughest of all.

Naturally smooth

Some things are naturally smooth.
The leaves of an apple tree are quite
smooth, but not completely smooth.
The skin of an apple feels smoother.

The insides of these shells are smoother than the outsides. Some of the pebbles are also quite smooth. Which pebbles are the smoothest? (Answer on page 31.)

Smooth cloth

Silk feels very smooth when you rub it on your skin. The ribbon in this girl's hair is almost as smooth as the silk scarf.

Sheets are smoother than **blankets**. Blankets keep you warm, but a smooth sheet against your skin is more comfortable.

Smooth and hard

Metals are very hard. They can also be very smooth. All of these things are made of smooth metals. Which object is made of silver? (Answer on page 31.)

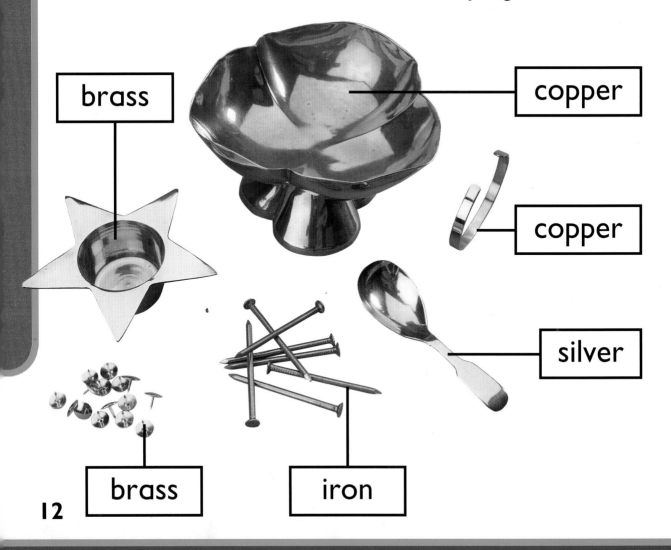

brass

copper

copper

silver

brass

iron

Other materials can be smooth
too. The box is made of plastic.
The bottle is made of glass and
the cup is made of china.

Easy to clean

Smooth things are easier to clean than rough things. Sinks, pans and plates are all smooth. It is easy to wash them.

A pan scrubber is rougher than a cloth or sponge. The rough side is better for rubbing away food that is stuck to a plate.

Making something smooth

When two rough **surfaces** rub together, they become smoother. This wall has a rough patch. Rubbing it with rough sandpaper will make it smoother.

These shiny pebbles have been tumbled in a special machine. As they tumbled, they rubbed against each other. This made them smooth and **polished**.

Slipping and sliding

Smooth **surfaces** are usually very slippery. Ice is smooth and very slippery. Unless you are used to skating, it is hard to stay on your feet.

This boy is sliding down a shiny metal slide. Metal is not as slippery as ice, but it is much more slippery than wood.

Wet surfaces

Water is smooth. So wet **surfaces** are more slippery than dry ones. This floor is wet. People must be careful not to slip on it.

Do not run around the edge of a swimming pool. It is often wet and slippery. These children need to walk carefully.

Treads

These trainers have a deep **tread** cut into the soles. The tread makes the sole rough. Treads stop your shoes from slipping on smooth ground.

Rubber **tyres** have treads cut into them too. The treads help the wheels to grip the ground. Mountain bikes have deep treads to grip the slippery tracks.

Friction

When two rough **surfaces** rub against each other, they stick together a little. The stickiness is called **friction**. Friction stops things sliding.

Push a box along the floor. When you let go, it soon slows down and stops. Friction between the box and the floor slows the box down.

Testing surfaces

Rough **surfaces** make more **friction** than smooth surfaces. This boy is testing different surfaces. He finds that the rougher the surface, the greater the friction.

He pushes one car along a wooden floor. Then he pushes another car along a carpet. He measures how far each car has travelled. Which car has travelled further? (Answer on page 31.)

Using rough surfaces

These table mats are made of a material called **raffia**. Raffia is rough and the mats are bumpy. This means that plates do not slip off them easily.

The pages of this book are rougher than most books. This person cannot see. Instead she feels the pattern of dots to read the words. This writing is called **Braille**.

Glossary

bark the outer layer of a tree

blanket warm bed cover made of wool or similar material

Braille a sort of writing that uses dots to make words

friction the force that stops two surfaces sliding easily across each other

polished when a surface has been rubbed with wax or something similar, until it is shiny

raffia material made from the leaves of palm trees. Raffia is used to make hats and baskets.

silk a fine thread made by the caterpillars of the silk moth. Silk thread is woven into cloth.

surface the outside layer of something

tread deep grooves and ridges cut into a rubber or plastic surface

tyre the rubber layer that covers part of a wheel

Answers

page 9
The white pebbles are the smoothest pebbles.

page 12
The spoon is made of silver.

page 28
The car on the wooden floor has travelled further.

Index

Titles in the *My World of Science* series include:

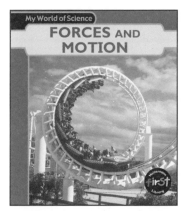

Hardback   0 431 13700 5

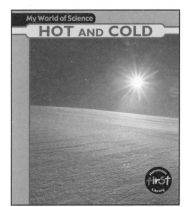

Hardback   0 431 13715 3

Hardback   0 431 13712 9

Hardback   0 431 13704 8

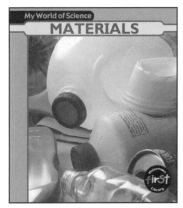

Hardback   0 431 13701 3

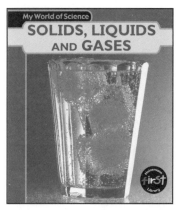

Hardback   0 431 13702 1

Hardback   0 431 13714 5

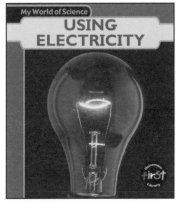

Hardback   0 431 13716 1

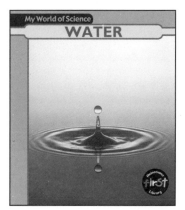

Hardback   0 431 13703 X

Find out about the other titles in this series on our website www.heinemann.co.uk/library